BLACK SWAN

The Twelve Lessons of Abandonment Recovery

Featuring: *The Allegory of the Little Girl on the Rock*

by Susan Anderson

rock foundations press

Huntington, New York

BLACK SWAN: The Twelve Lessons of Abandonment Recovery

Published by

rock foundations press

P.O. Box 2307—Suite B
Huntington, New York, 11743-2307

Book Design by Anne-Marie Johnstone – amjsun@aol.com

ISBN 0-9673755-1-7

Library of Congress Catalogue Card Number: 99-93501

Warning: While this book is designed to enlighten and enter-
tain, it may be disturbing to some people sensitive to certain
emotional themes. It portrays a little girl who has been abandoned by her father, left in the woods. Although this book may
have a therapeutic impact in helping adults get in touch with
their feelings and find a direction for positive change, it is not
a substitute for individuals who require professional counsel to
ensure their well being and stability. Those interested in en-
hancing the abandonment recovery process are encouraged to
employ additional aids such as support groups, sponsors, men-
tal health professionals, and/or other related self-help books.
(See also *The Journey From Abandonment To Healing* by Susan Anderson.)

For additional information about products and services, contact the author's website **www.abandonmentrecovery.com.**

Parents and Teachers:

This book is <u>not</u> intended for children. It is an allegorical treatment of a sensitive issue, designed to help adults internalize a message of healing.

TABLE OF CONTENTS

BEGINNING

BLACK SWAN is a symbol for healing. This book provides emotional and spiritual guidance to those struggling with the issue of abandonment. You may be in the throes of a devastating heartbreak and loss, or have trouble finding someone to love, or insecurities from the past may interfere in your current relationships. You may be a searching adoptee, recently widowed, or someone still pining for an old love. Your childhood wounds may still impinge. Some may already be involved in a twelve step program, attempting to deal with the impact of unresolved abandonment—the source of all our addictions, compulsions, and distress. The *Twelve Lessons* offer a path for recovering from our old wounds as well as the new.

I began writing this book as I was going through a painful loss in my own life. The irony of my circumstances was that I had specialized in helping people overcome abandonment for over twenty years in my practice as a psychotherapist. I had perused the self help books and professional literature over the years in search of supplementary material for my clients. Nothing I found was able to speak to the intensity of the experience or provide substantial direction for healing. Now, urged by my own experience, I decided to write my own account to plumb the depths of the abandonment wound and come to a better place of understanding than before.

At that time, a black swan suddenly appeared in the harbor where I took my walk each day. I was captivated by his graceful silhouette as he made his way through the community of white swans, a dignified presence among them. The sight of the lone swan sailing across the waters inspired me to reach into my deepest experiences and create an allegorical tale revealing the *Twelve Lessons of Abandonment Recovery.*

The techniques described in these pages were inspired not just by my own personal experience, but by having seen countless abandonment survivors perform the miracle of recovery. I observed what methods worked for them and what worked for me. The *twelve lessons* are the actual twelve steps involved in recovery from abandonment.

Through many years of working with people, I found that a most effective way to internalize messages of growth and recovery is through metaphor. Storytelling appeals to the imagination, creativity and healing powers within. A well told tale captivates our interest and bypasses the internal gate keepers—the unconscious mechanisms that keep us locked in patterns of self sabotage. Caught off guard we open the door to internal change. Throughout history, philosophers and healers have conveyed their wisdom through fables and parables. Handed down through the ages, these stories have instilled hope and direction to aid in human growth and development.

BLACK SWAN gets its healing message across through the medium of storytelling. The tale features *a little girl on the rock* who serves as a symbol for the losses and heartbreaks, large and small, we have all experienced. Through her, we get in touch with our oldest and truest feelings left over from childhood. As we watch her progress, we discover our own path of recovery—from our current wounds and those still lingering from the past.

The severing of an adult attachment bursts the old wounds, flooding us with fears and insecurities whose origins we may no longer recall. Abandonment creates a real emotional crisis with the impact to alter life-direction. The ending of a relationship provides a new beginning. Through this painful experience, profound personal growth emerges. As we follow the steps of healing, we are able to tend to needs not met that have been interfering in our lives all along. We heal from the inside out.

My work with both adults and children allowed me to explore the scope and dimension of the abandonment wound and appreciate the special nature of its grief. Through trial and error, we discovered techniques to maximize the potential for growth at each stage. Recovery follows a sequence, a series of steps taking us through a cycle of loss and renewal.

Abandonment is a complex human issue, its wound deeply entrenched in fear and insecurity. Without recovery, abandonment can linger beneath the surface, undermining self esteem and sabotaging future relationships. The tools of healing help to reverse this injury. We build a new sense of self, increase our capacity for love, and find greater life and relationships than before.

BLACK SWAN is a form of biblio-therapy, a self-help tool. You gain emotional benefit by reading and enjoying the story. Afterwards the text serves as a reference for the *Twelve Lessons of Abandonment Recovery*—a reference to be reviewed. It contains instructions and examples for following the exercises, a blueprint for changing your life. The lessons take us through the recovery process step by step—from discovering our center, to developing a new sense of self, and finally to making a new connection.

PART ONE

Little Girl on the Rock

A little girl and her daddy go into the woods to pick a bouquet of wild flowers. They follow a path all the way to the brook where they are immersed in the richness of the forest. Daddy walks the little girl across a log and onto an island in the water. He lifts her up and sets her atop a giant rock. "You stay here," he says, "and I'll go pick us some huckleberries for lunch."

The little girl clasps her hands. "Don't go far, Daddy," she begs.

"I won't," promises the daddy. He makes his way back across the log and into the forest as the little girl studies the back of his red shirt to keep track of him. He is momentarily hidden, first behind this tree and then behind that one. Suddenly there is no sign of red at all.

Perched atop the giant rock on the island, the little girl begins calling to her daddy, hoping he is right nearby only teasing her. "Daddy, I'm here," she calls. "Daddy, where are you?" But after a while she can't hold back her terror. She screams into the forest with all her might. But the forest is silent.

As night falls the little girl is frozen with fright on the cold hard rock. She is aware of the slithering sounds of snakes and other woodland animals creeping about. She tries not to move. She doesn't want to alert the creatures to her position high atop the rock. But soon she succumbs to terror once again. "Daddy, Daddy, Daddy," she cries into the now pitch black darkness. "Mommy! Daddy!" The forest remains distinctly silent except for the menacing sounds of the animals lurking about.

Lying on her side, she is uncomfortable in her soiled clothing. She draws her knees up to her chest to hug them, trying to make herself into a ball to try to get warm. Eyes open, unblinking, she keeps a steady vigil throughout the night, afraid she will be eaten.

Morning eventually arrives, its first rays of light, dim and ghastly. The illumination is hideous; it heightens her awareness of her position atop the rock. The brook rushes by. The surrounding forest is dense and enveloping.

The little girl knows that she cannot stay on the rock or she will surely die. The snakes will get her or she will starve or freeze or be frightened to death. She knows she must get down. But how? She is way up high and the sides are too steep, too steep to slide down. She thinks about jumping. But she will get hurt. Maybe Daddy will come, she hopes. But the waiting is too torturous to endure any longer. She will just have to take her chances and try to let herself fall off the rock. It is the only thing left to do. But she knows she has to be careful not to break too many bones— especially not her arms and legs. If she survives, she will need them to crawl across the log to get to the forest floor. If she can fall the right way, she tries to reassure herself, she might make it.

Finally, she takes a big gulp of air and faces certain pain as she executes her fall.

It is a terrible, hard, crushing thud on reaching the ground. She feels herself alive but is not glad of it for she cannot move. Her eyes are squeezed shut. Her side is aflame with pain. Finally she finds her voice and whimpers to the lonely forest of silent trees. "Help me, help me," she cries.

She attempts to draw her arms around her body and rock herself for comfort. This mobility is only an impulse at first, but soon she is able to free her hands to brush off the pebbles and debris from the abrasions and gashes along her hip and leg.

As morning sunlight intensifies, she feels the pain in her side get stronger and sharper, but soon she is able to carefully move her limbs. She works at this sensation and finally pushes herself up and, after a wobbly first start, begins to balance herself. Next, she begins to manage her way, in spite of searing pain, carefully down the log which spans the gushing brook. As she painfully inches along, she hopes she can find her daddy, if only she can make it to edge of the forest.

She finally arrives at the shore and begins to work her way into the thick forest. She is holding her hip and limping, trying to follow the direction her daddy's red shirt had taken when he disappeared.

At times she sees a flash of red and follows it into the thickets, veering off the path. The patches of red turn out to be illusory—the tip of a bird wing, the blushing petal of a woodland flower. Her heart sinks with disappointment. And then she thinks she sees red again and rushes deeper into the wilderness in pursuit.

By now she has abandoned the network of narrow foot paths that meander this way and that throughout the dense woods. Hunger pangs seize her stomach, and she stops her frantic search to take stock of her position. She turns around in all directions. Nothing seems familiar. No paths to follow. She calls out in terror. "Daddy! Mommy! Where are you? Help me!"

She spends the next several days dazed and bewildered, calling out to her absent parents, trying to find her way through the wilderness. Her world is filled with terror, stomach cramps, and cold. She continues searching, eats huckleberries, and sleeps on top of logs. All she wants is to find her daddy and mommy and go home. Her heart pounds when she thinks she might never find them. She shakes her head to make the thought go away. She can't be lost forever!

One morning, the chirping of a bird gently awakens her. Freckles of sunlight sprinkle across her forest bed. Soon the bird flies off and the little girl clears sleep from her eyes as she watches him disappear into the sky. She is suddenly struck with the realization that she must find her way back to the brook. Then she won't feel so lost, she reasons. She would only have to walk alongside it, first in one direction, and then perhaps the other, in order to find the giant rock where Daddy left her. From there she might be able to find the path that leads back through the woods, up the hill, and to her house at the edge of the forest. She has walked it many times, but always with her mommy or daddy. Now she will have to find her way home alone. It is her only chance.

Yes, she must find the island with the rock. It will be

a starting point. She remembers that the ground slopes downhill toward the brook. She attempts to follow the subtle downward trend of the forest floor. After a trial, wandering along, she senses a definite slope under her feet, and her heart rushes as she favors it. She moves downward, descending gradually for a long while.

And then the sky brightens ahead. She hears it. The brook!

She runs to greet the water's edge, there to walk along it jubilantly. She has found something familiar. The direction she has chosen feels right. After an hour or so she senses familiar terrain and keeps going, her steps quickening as she sees the log up ahead. There it stands—the giant rock on the island glistening in the sunlight. Her heart pounds in recognition.

The path stretches before her—the same path she and her daddy had taken to the brook. Would she have enough time to find her way back home before it gets dark?

She tries the main path, her limbs rushing along. But it soon forks in opposite directions and she can't remember which one to take. She picks the path that goes left, but it soon dwindles down to nothing. She is lost again. But this time she has not lost her sense of the brook. She knows how to follow the forest's descent back to the brook, and then back again to the original setting. The rock shall be her beginning point to start anew, from which she can find the right combination of paths, no matter how many trials it takes. She will find her way home.

Toward the end of day, she sees a familiar path in the dusk. It leads her straight up a hill. She recognizes a patch of telescope plants she and her brother and sister used to play with. Anticipation rushes through her chest. She sees the bramble bushes, the ones she got stuck on before, and up ahead, the skunk cabbage with its familiar, pungent aroma. She rushes to make her way up this familiar hill. Up ahead she sees the summit with its tall trees that have vines just right for swinging, cascading downward. Seeing her way through these friendly old trees, she greets the final path that leads directly to her house.

And there it is, right up ahead. Home. She runs toward it just as darkness falls.

She rushes to the front door, ready to throw herself upon it. "Daddy! Mommy!" she is about to call. But just then she sees something that makes her heart stop. Her breath is sucked back. It is the big bay window. Through it, she sees the dining room all aglow with candles. There sits her whole family around the table smiling and laughing. They are all there—her mommy and daddy and brother and sister—everybody together and happy without her !

She staggers backward from the sight, the overwhelming truth catching in her chest. She has been abandoned.

She creeps further back like a wounded animal, re-moving herself to the edge of the forest. Her heart is frozen in terror but she does not cry out. She knows the danger is real. There, under cover of encroaching darkness, she keeps vigil upon her house. The lugubrious black of night closes in on her.

She gropes for leaves and pine needles in the dark-ness to make a place to lay down. Enveloped in darkness, she listens to the rustling sounds of hungry animals in the woods around her. Her heart pounds and her mind races. She remains with the awful knowledge of her abandon-ment, her chest hurting, until daybreak.

When it is light enough, her heart stricken with grief, the little girl returns to the forest edge to watch over her family, attempting to observe its activity under cover of dense forest. There she sees Mommy and Daddy coming and going, her brother and sister in tow. She remains vigi-lant all day for signs of them, her pulse quickening and stomach sinking at each sighting.

At night she carefully sneaks bits of food to eat from the garbage left over from her family's meals and takes scraps of paper towels and thrown out things to make her woodland bed more comfortable. She is grateful for any remnants of them.

As nights go by she has acquired many articles of warmth and comfort from her family's garbage. Then one day the little girl observes a moving van pull up to her house, and she watches Mommy and Daddy load up all of the familiar family possessions. Her brother and sister are gleeful and excited. Finally, Mommy's and Daddy's arms circle round the children and off they drive in the moving van. Daddy gives the horn a triumphant toot as they depart.

She feels her chest pounding as she watches them disappear up the street, but she does not cry out for them. Nor does she abandon her vigil upon the house. She waits minute by minute for their return.

A whole week goes by, but the house remains vacant. The waiting is unbearable. Finally she advances out of her resting place in the forest. She walks up to her house and attempts to enter the front door. It is locked up tight.

She circles the house to peer in all of the windows to witness empty rooms, dust, and discarded debris. She stares into the emptiness of her old bedroom. She vaguely registers the absence of her teddy, her dolls, her bed.

Then, after a while, thinking nothing, feeling nothing, she walks away—not back to the forest, but as far away as she can from all that she has just experienced. Vacantly, she walks across the lawns, up one street and down the next, and onto the next and up and down through streets she has never walked before. She is barely aware of the traffic getting louder and louder as she wanders through its din.

As night falls, she comes to a railroad station and decides to sleep along the tracks. By early morning, someone has noticed her sleeping among the discarded debris. She is taken to the police station where they are putting their hands upon her and moving their mouths and making sounds that she does not attempt to distinguish.

She is taken to a shelter, then to a foster home, followed by another and another, as the weeks and months go by. There is a succession of staring people intruding into her silence with words and faces. But she has learned to find the warmth and comfort of her own urination and defecation in the many beds she is lain. Each night she keeps vigil upon the doorways and studies the cracks of light long into the nights in all of the various and strange houses that she has been placed in.

She doesn't notice the seasons change, or that her hair is growing, or that she herself is growing. And then one day she is taken to a residential facility. She barely notices the many children who gape at her as she is taken on tour through the old stone building where she is to live among them. There, as she makes her way down the halls and through the various rooms, still more people ask her where she is from and what her name is—questions she cannot answer, let alone find the will to speak.

Nor, when she is finally left at the residence, does she care to eat with the other children in the dining room. For her, there are no others. No one seems to be really there. No one seems real. When she is hungry, she steals food left over on the children's plates or out of the garbage and takes it to a corner in the kitchen by the garbage cans, there to eat under the counter.

Afterward, she beds down in the laundry piles. She is always forcibly led back to the dormitory and lain in bed. She does not remain, each night sneaking back to the rags and the laundry again and again, seeking comfort and warmth from her own bodily excretions.

Sometimes the other children hit her when she takes their food and call her 'stupid' and other bad names. Sometimes they push her away from them and punch her and tell her she smells. But she does not cry, for she cannot really feel them or hear them.

Many more months go by and finally an event occurs which feels familiar and real. She hears a woman crying, long and deep, from a distance. Soon it fills her ears, awakening her whole body to its tones. Finally a woman appears in the doorway, wiping her eyes. She approaches the little girl, crouching down and taking her by the hand. "Come with me, little one," says the woman wiping tears from her eyes with the hem of her long flowing skirts. Her voice is gentle.

The little girl does not see the woman clearly, for her eyes are not used to focusing. But she follows along in the vague indentation of softness and allows herself to be taken, letting her hand stay curled inside the woman's. She can smell her warmth and feel the gentleness wrapped around her hand.

She thinks of nothing, and does not resist as the woman helps her into her winter hat and coat, leading her out the big doors onto the large sprawling lawn where an apple orchard stands in the distance surrounded by Canadian geese. The woman stands back for a moment and says, "I'm going to take you to the water which is just down that way." She is pointing through the orchard to the sea beyond.

The little girl draws back from the woman's hand.

"Are you afraid of those trees, my darling? Then I won't take you that way," the woman says softly. "I will take you the long, open way, around the orchard and through the open meadow instead." And she draws the little girl along gently. "I want to introduce you to someone, someone very special," says the woman as they walk along. "See, you're doing fine." They slowly make their way to the water.

The little girl lets her hand relax and leaves it folded inside the woman's as they walk along. "We're almost there," says the woman. "See down there? That's where you'll meet the black swan."

PART TWO

The Twelve Lessons

Lesson one

The little girl is led to the water's edge where a dark, graceful curve on the horizon glides through the water, heading toward a flock of white swans who make room for its passage. It is a black swan who sails through them, gracefully turning this way and that, until he approaches the little girl at the water's edge, calling her by a new name.

"Amanda," says the swan. "You must find a spot within yourself so that I can speak with you."

The little girl is sitting on a log next to the woman whose arm circles round her. She lowers her head and begins to go inside. She searches within herself for a spot amidst the disarray and dread that reside within.

"Take your time," says the swan. "You must find the spot right in the center."

The skirt of the woman begins to flutter in the breeze as she fades silently into the background beside the little girl.

The little girl takes her hand from inside the woman's and places it over her own heart. She closes her eyes, feeling the woman's skirts fluttering across her knees.

"Open your eyes inside of your heart," says the swan, "and listen to me."

The little girl begins to cry out from within herself. "It hurts inside," she says.

"Yes, inside is where your feelings are," says the swan, "but you must go through your feelings all the way to their very center to find your listening space so that you can hear what I have to say."

"But it hurts! Daddy, Mommy, where are you? Please come and take me home!"

"You must go all the way inside, Amanda, to the place where you exist all by yourself. Your parents are not here with you now. In this moment you are alone, as we are all alone. For the moment, accept your aloneness. It is your surviving self."

"I can't. It's awful," weeps the little girl from her heart.

"You must go through the awfulness all the way to its very center. In the very center lives an aloneness that isn't awful anymore. It is an aloneness we all share. Can you find it?"

The little girl closes her eyes once more. She burrows deeply within herself, pressing her hands against her heart. The woman's arm is warm and gentle around her.

"It isn't awful, is it, Amanda? In the center, aloneness just is. It is reality. It is your reality as well as mine. It is a sacred place, an alone place just for you," says the swan, beginning to make a turn in the water. "It will be your special place to come to each time we meet."

The little girl hears the flutter of the swan's wings and slowly opens her eyes. She can see his neck stretch upward as he gracefully turns a full circle. "I'm going to go for now," says the swan, "but I will always be here when you need me. Practice finding your sacred spot within, Amanda, will you?"

She watches the swan turn this way and that as he glides gracefully away. "Come," says the woman, taking the little girl's hand in hers. "We'll return soon."

Lesson two

The day finally comes when the woman is supposed to take the little girl. There is a knot in her stomach as she waits. It is hard. She is waiting. She hurts inside her body from all of the waiting. She is afraid she will never see the woman again, that she is never coming back, that she will never see the black swan again. She places her hands over her heart and closes her eyes and hopes. And then a warm and gentle feeling comes with the flowing of soft skirts and she feels the knot in her stomach subside.

She is taken by the hand and led once again out the big doors to the lawn and past the Canadian geese milling about the apple orchard, pecking through the remains of snow. "Come with me, precious one," says the woman with soft, watery eyes and flowing skirts that flutter softly against her. They continue their walk hand in hand across the meadow and down the slope to the water.

The black swan is there again far out in the water, gliding toward the little girl. As he approaches, the other swans gracefully turn away making room for him. With a gentle swoop of his long neck he drifts through them and arrives at the shore line.

"How are you today, Amanda?" asks the swan.

The little girl settles on the log beside the woman. She places her hands over her heart.

"That's right, Amanda, go inside," says the swan. "Find your sacred space so you can hear what I have to say."

"It still hurts inside," she says. "Why did my daddy do this to me?" she cries from her heart.

"It is good that you are finding your feelings. It is part of discovering your center."

"But I want my daddy!" says the little girl.

"He is not here with you now, Amanda. And you feel the wound that he left. You do not have to let anyone into your center who brings bad feelings. You must push the person who has wounded you out of your center, Amanda. Push the wounder out so you can feel safe inside your sacred space."

The little girl feels the woman's skirts flutter against her. She begins to burrow down within herself, but once again she comes upon a strong feeling. "Why must people be mean to me?" she cries out. "Tell them to stop hitting me and yelling at me."

"You can push those who wound you out, Amanda. Inside your special alone space, only you are in command. Push the wounders out."

"But how?" cries the little girl.

"All you need is your imagination to push them all out. The space inside of you is sacred—safe and free."

The little girl's hands are still resting on her heart, but she turns them so that her palms are facing outward.

"Push them out, Amanda, and imagine a place inside of you that is free of bad feelings."

The little girl's palms begin pushing away from her chest.

"That's right, Amanda. Push the wounders out. Keep them out of your center and don't let them in."

The little girl feels the woman's skirts blowing gently against her and smells her warmth as she pushes the palms of her hands away from her chest.

"You must practice this when the bad feelings come. Find the sacred space inside that is all yours and only yours and keep it safe."

The little girl slowly opens her eyes as she hears the swan beginning to make his turn in the water. "I will be here when you need me," he calls, swimming back out to the gathering of white swans who make room for his return.

Lesson three

I
t has been a while since the little girl has seen the woman, but today is the day. The waiting is still hard. She is afraid the woman has left her. But this time when she closes her eyes, she places her hands out-turned from her chest as the feelings come. She pushes with her hands, trying to push bad feelings away.

Suddenly through the door comes the woman who crouches down next to the little girl and helps her on with her sweater, looking at her with her soft, liquidy eyes. The little girl feels relieved as she is led once again past the budding apple orchard to the water's edge.

She feels her heart flutter as she sees her beautiful

black swan approaching. From way out on the horizon he sails gracefully, trailed at a distance by two white swans. He dips his long, beautiful neck in the water as he approaches the little girl.

"How are you, Amanda?" comes his familiar voice. "Are you learning how to push the wounder out and keep your center safe inside?"

The little girl makes herself a comfortable place to sit on the shore, tucking herself into the woman's gentle arm to smell her warmth and feel her skirts blowing softly against her knees.

"Yes," she says, placing her hands over her heart, "but I am still afraid inside."

"Then it is time for you to learn how to use the moment," says the swan.

"The moment?" asks the little girl.

"The moment of now. Now is where all your power is. It is the way out of fear. And you have the tools to find it," says the swan. "Are you ready for me to show you the way out of being afraid?"

The little girl closes her eyes and begins to go inside. A strong feeling comes swiftly. "But I'm afraid something bad's going to happen to me!" she beseeches her precious swan.

"Fear is of the future, Amanda, and we cannot do anything about the future. We have no control over it because it doesn't exist yet. There is only now. The past and future may seem very big, but the biggest part is always now.   Now is where reality lives, and all of your fears, Amanda, are about the future—an imagined place."

"But I am afraid NOW," challenges the little girl.

"Go to the center of your fear, Amanda, so I can help you find the oasis between past and present—the ever-flowing wellspring of now."

The little girl draws a breath and nestles into the woman's arm.

"The moment is there, just waiting to be recognized, and you already have the tools you need to find it, Amanda. They are your eyes and ears and nose and skin and heart and mind.   But now you must learn to use these senses in a special new way, a way that brings you out of your fear of the future and into the now," says the swan. "And I will show you how."

The little girl burrows within herself.

"Open your ears, Amanda.   What can you hear in this moment?"   The swan waits to let the sound of his own voice dissipate so that background noises can flow in.

The little girl tilts her head so she can listen carefully.

"Can you hear insects?" he asks, nearly whispering.

She squeezes her eyes tighter and listens.   "Almost, yes."

"Can you hear anything else?"

She listens intently and finally speaks: "The little waves trickling against the pebbles."

"That is good," says the swan. And after a while he continues. "Open your eyes and see what you can see right here in this moment. Tell me what comes in first."

She slowly opens her eyes. "I see you."

"That is good. Can you see the light itself?" he asks.

"Yes," says the little girl, her eyes moving to the larger scope of water and sky.

"Can you see its patterns in the sky and special designs upon the water?"

"Yes," she says, a tiny smile turning up her lips.

"That is good. Now can you feel anything in your body?"

The little girl pauses for a while. "I feel my stomach pumping," she says.

"Good. Can you feel anything against your skin?"

"I think I am sitting on a pebble. I can feel it."

"You are feeling the moment and that is good. And what can you smell?"

She inhales deeply and then wrinkles her nose. "I smell seaweed, I think."

"Yes," says the swan, turning in the water. "Bring all the life you can through your senses. They are the moment's great tools. Use them to open your floodgates to the life all around you."

The little girl's face is relaxed, but once again she comes upon a feeling. "I'm still scared," she whimpers. "I'm afraid I'll always be alone!" she cries. "What will become of me!" She feels the woman's arm circle around her waist.

"You have lost the moment, Amanda. Remember, it is only in the future that we fear our separateness. But as we return to the split moment of now, we no longer fear our aloneness; we command it. In the moment, aloneness is nothing to fear; it is only a reality we all share."

"But what if I never see Mommy and Daddy again?" cries the little girl.

"We have no control over the future or other people, Amanda. In the moment, the future gets to take care of itself one moment at a time. The future is nothing but the present waiting to be commanded when we get there. As we move forward, it is always now."

The little girl shakes her head. "But my daddy left me!" she cries.

"And when you got through that very bad time, it was in the present, wasn't it?"

"Yes, but I was so scared!"

"You didn't know how to use your tools in a special way to help you not be afraid, but you still got through it, one moment at a time, didn't you?" insists the swan, swirling around in the water. "Imagine how much better it will be when you learn to use your ears and eyes and skin as special gifts of serenity and peace. Each sense is a different window to bring you a different view of the moment."

The swan dips his long head into the water and comes up again and looks upon the little girl who is sitting on the shore, shaking her head. "It is very easy to get distracted from being in the moment and slip back into worries and fears and other things."

The little girl nods.

"But you can always return to the oasis of the moment. Find the moment for me again, Amanda. Can you bring in anything from your senses that feels good, anything that is beautiful?"

The little girl closes her eyes. "I feel a breeze against my face."

"Yes, Amanda, as long as you are concentrating on that sensation, you have left your fears about the future and your sadness over the past and entered the moment. Is it not bountiful? The now is always there for you anytime you need it," says the swan, turning in a circle, "as I will always be here. Remember," he calls behind him, "the moment is a refuge from fear. You must practice it as often as you need it," he says and glides away.

The little girl and the woman return slowly up the slope and back to the residence as the sun sprinkles across the meadow and butterflies light upon the taller grasses amidst rustling sounds and tingling breezes.

Lesson four

One evening after an early summer rain, the little girl ventures out of her usual corner in the kitchen to follow the children out to the yard. There, standing alone in the damp grass, she opens her eyes to the lightning bugs for the first time. They are flickering in the dark. At a distance, she watches the other children catching them. She wishes she could cup one of the fire-flies in her hands to study its magic, as the other children are doing. But her arms remain hanging at her sides.

That night, as usual, she is lifted from her rags in the corner of the pantry and put back in bed in the dormitory.

"No!" she cries as the blankets are placed around her.

"It will be okay," comes the reassuring voice of the house mother. "You must try to stay. Try it for a while."

This time the little girl does not attempt her usual retreat to the rag pile. Instead, she remains in her bed thinking about the lightning bugs and wondering why they must die so quickly. They are of the moment. She thinks of the swan and opens her eyes wide to bring in what there is to see. She studies the shadows forming against the windows outside. Then she strains her ears to bring in what she can hear. To her wonder, she deciphers the low murmurings of the night people creeping about downstairs in the kitchen.

As her mind wanders into the sensations of life abounding in the night, she falls off to sleep in her very own bed.

Each new morning she wakes up in her bed, yet each early morning sunlight brings an uneasy feeling in her stomach that does not want to go away. She practices finding the moment to help her get through. Using her ears and eyes and nose and skin, she begins to notice many new things here and there. One day for instance, she notices flowers that seem to have popped up in the yard overnight. She likes their name: Snapdragons. Another day, she spies a familiar bird—it seems to have come to her from the past. It is bright red and lands on a branch right outside her window. Its so red, so sudden, so beautiful—it startles her, causing her heart to pound. One night she listens to the bomb blasts of a big thunderstorm rattling through the old stone house.   She observes the other children in their fright and amazement and feels her own excitement mingle in. Another day she notices the lush green carpet of lawn that seems to have wrapped itself around the old stone house while she wasn't even noticing. It seems to have brought gentler temperatures.

But between these moments, she is waiting—waiting and worrying and trying to push out the bad feelings that come. She waits for that special day when she gets to see the black swan again. While she waits, she practices all that she is learning—to find her center, push away bad feelings, and find the moment.

She has waited a long time, all the way until the gentle temperatures have turned into hot weather, to see her beloved swan. When at last she sees him, she can't hold back any longer. "I have nobody who loves me!" she cries. The woman, as usual, is by her side.

"You are facing your separateness, Amanda," comes his comforting voice. "And that is good."

"But I don't want to be separate!" cries the little girl. "I want my mommy and daddy to come back to me!"

"You can still love them and want them if you choose, but they are not here with you now. You are here now. You and I."

"But I need them!" cries the little girl from her heart, the woman's gentle arm encircling her. "And I always will!"

"Need is a feeling, Amanda. In truth, we don't need

any *one* person to survive. The world is full of people when we need them. They are called *others.*"

"But I only want my mommy and daddy," whimpers the little girl. "I want them to come and take me. If only you could understand!"

The swan pulls back into the water and opens his wings. "I, too, have longed for someone's return, Amanda. I, too, have known a wounder."

The little girl opens her eyes to see her beautiful swan arch his long neck. "Tell me," begs the little girl.

The swan moves gracefully to the shore line, swooping his head down, coming in close to the little girl. "Like you, I didn't think I could live without her," he continues in a soft voice. "I yearned for her to comfort me from the very wound she inflicted. But she could never be the one to comfort me. The wounder never can. Only finding the moment can do that."

"Who was your wounder?" asks the little girl.

"Swans mate for life, Amanda. You will notice I am alone. But I have survived the wounding, and so must you."

"Tell me more about her," begs the little girl, nestling into the woman's warm shoulder.

"She, like all wounders, became powerful just by wounding. She brought me to a feeling of insignificance and to pain. All I could do was marvel at her power to accomplish so mighty a task. I was reduced to helplessness, while she seemed to become more powerful, more valuable, and more beautiful for having vanquished me.   I could only worship my wounder," admits the swan. He turns gracefully toward the little girl. "But the pain this caused helped me find my will to survive and survive separately."

"How did you ever do that?" asks the little girl.

"To survive, I learned to breathe life into my separate self," says the swan, "just as you must do."

"But I will always love my mommy and my daddy," sighs the little girl.

"You don't have to stop loving them, or think unkindly of them to find your comfort. But you must learn to accept your separateness."

"I can't! It's too hard!"

"You're already beginning, Amanda. I will show you how to make it easier," offers the swan. "It just means using your imagination. Are you ready?"

The little girl nestles into the crook of the woman's arm and looks at the swan swooping his long neck into the water.

"Close your eyes and imagine your safe space within."

The little girl complies, feeling the breeze against her face.

"Imagine that your father is over there on the harbor front, Amanda," says the swan. "But he is turned away."

"Daddy!" cries the little girl in her heart.

"Pretend to get as far away from the wounder as you can. Go away, further and further out beyond the shoreline. Keep going until you can't see him anymore, until you are alone within the sea grasses. Imagine yourself feeling safe inside and completely separate. Exaggerate your separateness. Keep going, using your most confident stride to get further out to the open beach, to the furthest place you can see. Keep going and find a place where the sun sparkles most brightly in the sand, far away from everyone. Feel the peace and calm of being completely alone. All the way out there, feel your aloneness. Get inside the center of your aloneness," says the swan. He pauses to allow some silence to grow.

The little girl closes her eyes as she floats far away onto the sun drenched beach.

"Are you alone, Amanda?" asks the swan after a while.

"Yes," she says softly.

"That is good. Now use your tools to find the moment. Bring in the warmth of the sun as it bears down upon you. Imagine experiencing it just for yourself."

The little girl's face is relaxed as she basks in the sun. "Can you imagine a cool wind blowing across the shore bringing relief from the brilliant sun? Can you feel the sense of yourself from within, your stomach and heart alive with activity? Can you feel your power to bring in so much life through your senses just for your own sake?"

The little girl breathes deeply and turns her face up-ward.

"Yes, lift your face, Amanda. Give yourself to it. It is your separateness. You are celebrating it. Lift your face to the breezes of life around you. Open yourself to your whole-ness. You do not need the wounder now."

"Daddy," whimpers the little girl. But she remains basking in the calm.

"The wounder is far away, separate from you. He is back on the harbor front, Amanda. You never have to give him your power. Anytime you feel the pull against your power, use your imagination and go out to the furthest place you can imagine. Get as far away as you can and exaggerate your separateness. Go all the way out, away from everybody, where nature's most welcoming elements can be felt most intensely and imagine experiencing them alone, all for yourself. Know that you are whole—all by yourself."

The little girl begins to open her eyes as she hears the swan's motion in the water.

"Separate, Amanda," says the swan, making his turns, "so that you can become available to the love that is all around you. I will always be here when you need me."

Lesson five

The little girl imagines, as she awakens in her bed on certain mornings, that she is separate. It feels strange, but it also feels good sometimes. One morning she hears thunder and lightning and rain striking the roof. She decides to take a walk through the old stone house. It is her first lone exploration.

The other children have not seen her moving freely about before and shout to her as she enters the various hallways and rooms. She places her hands upon her heart and does not respond to their calls, but looks down and continues her lone parade, covering nearly the entire house.

During her next long awaited meeting with the swan, she tells him about her daring expedition, the woman, as always, by her side. "I feel very bad. The children don't like me," she says. "I wish I was special like you are."

"I am not special, Amanda."

"But you ARE special. You're special because you're the black swan."

"I am not special over anyone else," says the swan. "It is just by an act of nature that I happen to be black among white swans. It has nothing to do with being special."

"If a black swan isn't special," asks the little girl, "then, who is?"

"I am a lone center of the vast universe just like you are, just like everybody else," says the swan, swooping his neck into the water.

"But I'm not special at all. I'm plain. The other children don't like me."

"It's not about being special, Amanda. It's about being important to yourself."

"But the other children are better than me. I'm like garbage—people throw me away."

The swan flutters his wings. "Only you can do that to yourself. And only you can become important to yourself."

"But how?" asks the little girl.

"When I first came to these waters, Amanda, I was all alone. I was feared and hated by the other swans for being different. There were no other black swans at all and the other white swans rejected and ignored me. Then one day I found my way out to the most distant place I could find, just as I showed you, Amanda."

The little girl nestles into the woman's shoulder as she hears the swan tell his story.

"I went all the way out to the deepest waters, as far as I could get, way out into the sea. I overcame the currents with my own strength and made it all the way to the darkest ocean, away from everyone. I felt my aloneness. I got inside the center of it and felt the cold currents pass underneath me. Out there by myself, I faced my separateness for the first time. I felt the essence of being alive, just for my own sake. There was a feeling of peace and calm within me. I relished the chill of the wind through my feathers and listened with amazement to the sea gulls calling out to the universe. What I discovered was my power to experience my aliveness, alone as I was. My senses became my greatest gifts. They brought me life. The other swans were free to rebuke me if they liked."

"But you are respected," she challenges. "The other white swans make room for you, even follow you."

"Yes, they make room for me now and some even follow me. But it's not me they make room for now. It's the caring that I have for myself. It is the power over myself in the moment that they make room for."

"But I'm not special enough to have this power."

"Feeling the importance of being alive doesn't involve any special power. It has nothing to do with whether you're talented, or beautiful, or strong, or smart, or any of these things. These have nothing to do with experiencing one's existence. They are only attributes—the spokes of the wheel—not its center."

"But I have nothing!"

"You don't need anything special to feel the importance of being alive. If you want someone to tell you about your fine attributes, I am sure you will be told wonderful things, but you will have to go elsewhere for that. If you want to feel the importance of your own existence, I am here to help you," says the swan.

"But I'm not good enough."

"We are all good enough, Amanda, good enough to experience life. I will show you where to begin."

"But I am nobody!" cries the little girl.

"You have a name, Amanda. Say your name inside your center. Fill the whole space with your name. Pronounce it boldly and know that this is you. There is only one you, nobody like you, a separate person, you."

The little girl closes her eyes and burrows within herself, searching for her name. She can't remember it. She searches and searches. Finally she pronounces the name the swan calls her. "Amanda." But then a strong feeling comes. "It feels empty and sad inside!" She cries out across the water.

"Yes, Amanda, it will feel empty until you fill it with

things in life that have importance to you. Lift your chest a little bit and make it larger inside. Fill the whole space with your name."

The little girl lifts her chest and pronounces the name AMANDA within.

"Now you must think about what things in life you like. That's what your name will mean."

"But there is nothing I like!" cries the little girl.

"You have the tools to discover what you like, Amanda—your senses. At least you have already found out what you like through your taste buds, I'm sure."

"No, I haven't!" defies the little girl.

"Do you like ice cream?"

"It's too cold," protests the little girl.

"That is good to know. How about warm pie that's just come from the oven? Have you experienced that?"

"Hhmmm," says the little girl.

"What is your favorite flavor?"

The little girl looks at the swan dreamily. "Apple," she says.

"And that is good. It is a beginning. Next you can open your ears and decide what sounds you like to hear. The trickle of water? Music? The tinkle of laughter? And what games do you enjoy? Catching fireflies? Discover what pleases you out there in the world as a separate be-ing. And then go out and experience each thing. And as you do, know that it is because you are important. You must practice this and discover new things everyday. Fill yourself with what feels good and right. That is who you are, Amanda," says the swan, floating away. "I will be here any-time you need help filling yourself with life."

Lesson six

The little girl is inspired to find good things. She goes through the next week walking into places she has not been before. One day she appears in the gymnasium.

"You have finally decided to join us," the teacher says.

She bows her head. The other children are playing with the ball. It bounces hard against the wall. She hears the children shouting and holds her hands over her ears as she retreats to the doorframe. She says her name within herself to drown out the sounds. She knows she hates the sound of the ball and the shouting children. She knows she loves the meadows and the water and the sun and the warm smell of the woman and the soft pastel colors of her skirts and her beautiful black swan. Soon the noises of the game blend into the background and she thinks good thoughts.

When the whistle blows, the little girl takes her place in line for the first time with the other children. They do not shout at her or taunt her, but let her march all the way back with them to the old stone building, chests up, faces lifted to the breezes.

Throughout the weeks she waits for her chance to tell the swan of her adventures in the gymnasium and other places.

He commends her for her courage.

"But I'm still sad and miserable," complains the little girl to the swan. "I miss Mommy and Daddy all the time," she sighs. "I have good feelings sometimes, but I can't really play. Nothing feels good. Something is wrong with me."

"It is good that you are finding new things, and as you do, you will come across the sadness that is blocking your life. It is very real. You are facing the loss you have been through. And that is a good thing," says the swan.

The little girl feels the woman's skirts blow gently against her. "But it's not good. It hurts too much!" she cries.

"It is hard to go through the pain of loss," says the swan. "It is a great pain. A painful part of living and loving.

Many people have to go through it."

"But it makes me feel too bad and I can't do anything."

"The pain of loss is pulling you out of the moment,
Amanda. It pulls hard, like quicksand. Its pull brings powerful pain."

The little girl cries, letting her tears fall onto the
woman's skirts. "It won't go away."

"The pain of loss feels helpless because it comes
from the past, and the past is a place where we have no
power. We can't do anything about the past, because it is
already over. It no longer exists for us to control."

"But I don't want to live without my family!" cries the
little girl.

"Loss is very painful until we cross over. We must
cross over from the past to the present, from what we had
to what we have."

"But I miss my mommy and my daddy and I always
will."

"Yours is a difficult loss to face, Amanda. A difficult
reality can only be faced in the sheerest moment. It's too
big a job to be done once and for all. That's why the moment is such a special place."

"But I want Daddy to come back and get me!"

"Wanting and wishing will not bring him back. You
can accept this reality or fight it, Amanda. But fighting it

keeps you in the pain. Fighting it keeps you in a powerless place, filled with sadness. Your moment of life is now."

"But it is easy for you. You are not afraid," counters the little girl.

"I have a lot of fears, too, Amanda," says the swan, turning in the water. "I must face an uncertain future within unfamiliar waters. I know I will never see my home again and that I may have to die alone without a mate. I must use all of my will to cross over into my present life and ac-cept its realities—especially the reality of my aloneness and my strangeness among the others. But once I do this, I am filled with the power of existence, able to go on."

The little girl closes her eyes and draws in her breath.

"That's right, Amanda. Take a deep breath and be-long to the reality of now."

She lets her breath out slowly and evenly. "I am alone," she sighs. "But I don't want to be."

"It may not be the reality you want, but it is the real-ity you have, at least for the moment. If aloneness is the re-ality facing you, you must face it back."

"It hurts," whimpers the little girl.

"Yes," says the swan. "Pain is when the future and the past overlap and squeeze out the present. You must carve out a path between them. You must find the mo-ment. Get into its groove, Amanda, and fill yourself with the life all around you."

The little girl takes another deep breath and gazes out across the water, watching her beautiful swan make a full turn, and lets her breath out slowly.

"That's right, Amanda. Breathe in the present and breathe out the past. This is what you must practice. Open your ears and eyes and skin to the sounds of people who are all around you. Open your gills and breathe them in. Allow other people to fully enter the moment with you," says the swan, turning in the water, "as you have entered mine." He streams through the flock of white swans on his way out to the horizon.

Lesson seven

Summer draws to an end. This day is going to be different, decides the little girl as she looks out her window. She sees and hears the wind blowing against the tree branches. She walks downstairs to where the other children are eating. On most days, she peeks into the dining room, spying the food left over by the children and then curls up in her usual hiding position under the kitchen counter to devour stolen scraps of food in secrecy. If the house parents catch her, they coax her out of the corner and lead her back to the long dining table and try in vain to get her to sit down among the others.

This bright, blustery morning was going to be different. The little girl takes in a deep breath and practices finding the moment. First, with her ears, she hears the chatter of children in the dining room and the clatter of dishes in the kitchen. Then, with her eyes, she notices the light patterns coming through the windows. Finally, with her skin, she feels her arms being gently pulled by the house parents on either side. This time she is not resisting as they take her along into the dining room.

Suddenly a stripe of sunlight beams across the dining room table. It catches the silverware with a dazzling sparkle, delighting her for a moment. And then she notices that the other children seem peaceful sitting at the table. They are talking and laughing amongst themselves and not bothering her. She tugs at the sleeves of the house parents and bids them to sit her at the end of the table.

They go along with her request, looking with wonder at the little girl who is now sitting among the others. She doesn't look directly at the children, but she sits beside them nonetheless. The house parents sit on either side of the little girl for awhile, keeping her company. Then they tell her they must return to their duties.

The little girl stays put at the table. She is able to stay through the whole meal, even though she lacks appetite and doesn't touch her soup or milk or any of her food except for one bite of warm apple pie at the very end.

From then on, at each meal the little girl sits quietly at the end of the table among the other children, taking pieces of bread in her pockets for later.

A few weeks go by. It is the wee hours of the morning. The little girl suddenly awakens from a dream. Her heart pounds. The dream is about her parents. Their arms are around her. They are holding her tight. Their warmth feels so real, so loving. It is her first dream about them. And it is suddenly gone. Why must it be only a dream!

She tries to get back into the dream. She squeezes her eyes shut and concentrates real hard, but the dream won't come back. "Mommy and Daddy, why did you leave me?" she cries out. Her heart bursts with longing. She sinks in fear that they are never coming back. "Why? Why?" she sobs. She begins to drown in unbearable sadness and becomes afraid she will never get out. *'The moment. The moment,'* she thinks, her heart sinking with grief. She searches desperately for the moment. But the pain is too great. She is drowning in sorrow. But just as she is about to succumb to the worse of it, she imagines the swan's voice echoing through her chambers. *It's the loss, Amanda, the loss. It's the pain of loss. Face it. It hurts. It is life's greatest pain. It must be accepted, for it is real.*

"Don't leave me Mommy, Daddy! Please!" screams the little girl, pulling the covers over her head. "Don't leave me!" she cries and cries. "Somebody help me!"

She must have fallen asleep for she wakes up much later feeling fuzzy in her head and numb all over. She wanders into the music room. It is filled with children. At once they are all looking at her, but she is not afraid. She sits upon the floor among them. They turn their attention back to the song they are singing. The teacher asks them to hold hands in a circle. The little girl feels her hands being taken on either side. She feels uncomfortable inside her stomach, but does not pull away. She does not sing with the others, but lets her hands be held. She says her name within herself, lifting her chest, filling it with enough space for her name to be pronounced very loudly within. Her chest lifts almost all the way to her chin.

She stays through the music lesson, letting the children's voices filter in and around her, little tears falling down her cheeks.

Later when she is finally able to see her beloved swan, she tells him about her experience with the other children and beseeches him with her broken heart. It is a cry for love.

"I know that I am alone and that I was left on a rock to die!" she cries out, feeling the woman's arm circle round her. "And it hurts from my heart!"

"You are using great courage to face such a difficult reality as yours," says the swan. "And that is good."

"But it hurts! I want my daddy and mommy to love me!" pleads the little girl.

"Close your eyes, Amanda," says the swan, "so you can hear what I have to tell you. It will help you find warmth and comfort."

The little girl complies, wiping a whole face of tears.

"You are a child and a child is love. Press your hands over your chest until you can feel the warmth from your palms come into your heart. Can you feel it?"

The little girl presses and presses her palms over her chest and finally nods, yes.

"Imagine that this is the warm feeling of love."

"It's not love," she cries. "It hurts too much in my heart!"

"You must learn to use the love that is there now."

"But I don't have any."

"You have the capacity for love, just as I do, Amanda. Its warmth is waiting for you."

"But I don't know what to do!" she cries.

"You can begin with the idea of love, Amanda," says the swan. "Press the idea into your chest. Feel the warmth and hold the idea of love in your heart."

"But I don't want an idea," sobs the little girl. "I want love!"

"It will build, Amanda. Build to love. Someday you will share it with others."

"I can't be with people. I feel too strange and bad around them! And they are mean to me!"

The swan pulls back in the water. "I found my place among the others, even when they did not welcome me, when I found my capacity to love," he says. "My own love shone upon them, but I did not need them to receive it. My capacity for love was free for them to take or leave. Love has become my beacon, guiding my way through the giant ocean, ever since."

"But I don't have what you have," says the little girl.

"When my mate left me, Amanda, she took all the love in my heart with her. I had nothing left except yearning."

"Why did she leave?" queries the little girl, her hands crossed over her heart.

"I will tell you," promises the swan, arching his neck toward the little girl. "But I will wait until the idea of love has had time to gather inside you."

"Why can't you tell me now!" she begs.

"It is a sad story, Amanda," says the swan, "and I will need all of your warmth, your capacity for love, to receive it."

"What if I never get enough?" asks the little girl, gazing upon her swan.

"Love is something others can give you, but when they aren't able to, you can only get it back by creating it within yourself. All you need is imagination—and that you have. Close your eyes and feel the warmth from your hands. Imagine that all of the love in the world is yours."

"But it isn't!" cries the little girl.

"If you imagine it, it will be, Amanda," insists the swan.

The little girl lets her eyelids rest peacefully closed.

"Imagine the world as love, Amanda. You are enveloped in it. You are at the center of it all, as we all are—a spark of awareness—giving and receiving love," says the swan.

The little girl is pressing her palms upon her heart, but suddenly stops. "What is there to love?" she cries, tears falling down her face. "I am alone!"

"So am I, Amanda. But I love."

"Love what?" she demands.

"I love life. I love existence. I love me. I love the idea of love."

"That just goes in a circle!" she protests.

"It is the circle of love," agrees the swan. "A perfect circle. Love resides in the heart's imagination, Amanda," he says, moving toward her in the water. "Imagine that the warmth in your hands is love."

The little girl closes her eyes once again and burrows within herself, pressing warmth down into her heart.

"Remember, Amanda, love begins with your own idea, your own warmth, and it glows right inside your sacred space." The swan begins his turn in the water. "It takes lots of practice and I will give you time. I will be here when you are ready to share its warmth," he says, gliding through the gathering of swans who make room, out to the deepest waters.

Lesson eight

The little girl is sitting in the corner of the library, pressing her hands upon her heart. She is thinking about the woman's soft flowing skirts and gentle voice. She hopes the woman will come today. She has waited a long time to see her beloved swan.

Suddenly a boy comes into the room with a very determined stride. He is somewhat older and taller than the little girl and he walks right up next to her to look out the window.

GET AWAY, gestures the little girl with her hand. She is very afraid.

"I didn't touch you," shouts the boy.

She swings her hand, grazing the boy's leg.

He shoves a pile of books on the table. They go crashing to the floor beside the little girl. He slams the door on his way out of the room.

She begins punching the palm of her hand and feels the knot in her stomach tighten. She waits for the woman to come—waits and worries and hopes. She thinks about other things, but she keeps hearing the boy slam the door in her mind.

Finally she feels the familiar warmth of the woman's hand enclosing hers.

"Come precious one," says the woman, as together they meander out the big doors and down through the blooming apple orchard.   She can smell the fragrance. Soon they make their way to the water's edge.

The black swan approaches from the horizon, trailed by two white swans at a distance.   "How are you, Amanda?" asks the black swan, moving close to the little girl at the shoreline.

The little girl looks upon her swan. "People are mean to me," she says, her face wet with tears. "A boy came by and tried to upset me!"

"And you are very hurt, I see," says the swan.

"Yes," says the little girl. "And I don't know what to do."

"Have you tried using the golden rule?"

"But I want the boy to stop being mean!"

"The golden rule is not about how people treat you, but how you treat them, Amanda. Suppose the boy is unknowingly drawn to the warmth beginning to flow from your heart. How could he approach you without upsetting you?"

"Well," thinks the little girl, "he could just say hello and not look at me in a mean way and just stay away. And he better not stare at me."

"Then, this is how you must treat him tomorrow. You must say hello, not look at him meanly, and just stay away and not stare at him afterward."

"But he isn't nice to me. He doesn't deserve it."

"It's not about what he deserves. It's about following the simple rule of treating others exactly as you like to be treated."

"But he will still be mean to me," says the little girl.

"You cannot control how others behave or how they respond to you. You can only let others be who they are. But you can use the golden rule."

"Nobody cares what I do!" cries the little girl.

"Be the one to care. Try the golden rule on the boy. Treat him as you would like him to treat you."

"What if I am nice and he is mean to me?"

"Then walk away knowing you lived up to your own idea of how to act with people," says the swan. "And if he doesn't do something to make you feel good, then you must do something to make yourself feel good. Go off and experience something that brings you good feelings, something that brings warmth or pleasure."

"Nothing does," sighs the little girl.

"Remember when you admitted that you liked apple pie?"

The little girl nods and smiles, turning her palm upward toward the swan.

"Practice the golden rule, Amanda, and find things that bring you good feelings. It will help you be with others," he calls, dipping his long neck in the water as he goes.

Lesson nine

everal weeks later, the boy comes through the hallway again. This time he stays on the other side of the room, as far away as he can get from the little girl. She looks at him from her corner. Her heart pounds. She practices saying hello to him inside her mind, several times. Then she finally blurts out, "Hello, Jonathan!" Her stomach goes into a knot as she hears her own voice reverberate around the room. But she makes sure not to stare at him afterward. She listens as he moves toward the door.

"I didn't know you could talk," he calls to her as he lets the screen door bang shut behind him. Then he runs outdoors to play ball with the other boys.

The little girl runs down the hall to find the woman. Finally she sees her on the lawn and she rushes to her, pulling at her skirts. "The boy!" cries the little girl. "The boy!"

"You are finally talking," says the woman, putting her arm around the little girl, her skirts flowing against her side. "Come precious one, we will go see the swan."

When they arrive at the shoreline, the little girl watches her beautiful swan sail easily through the flock of white swans, turning gracefully this way and that, arriving to meet her. "Tell me what happened," he says.

"I was nice to the boy and he was mean to me," reports the little girl.

"That is good," responds the swan, making a full turn in the water. "Good that you were nice to him."

"But he was mean!" she cries.

"You felt he was mean," says the swan. "But if you keep treating others as you would like to be treated, eventually you will find those who will meet you halfway, people to feel safe with. These will be your friends."

"But then they will be mean to me and they will leave me!" she cries.

"People have their own life situations and problems and imperfections, just as you do, Amanda. They can only be who they are and sometimes it may not be what you want."

"But if I am nice to them, they should be nice to me," she insists.

"Giving to *give* is the idea, Amanda; giving to *get* doesn't work."

"But I want people to like me."

"Then you must like them."

"But it hurts if I am nice to someone and they are mean to me!"

"It is true that using the golden rule leaves you very open with people. To help protect yourself, you will need to bring the power of love into it."

"How do I do that?" asks the little girl. "They make me so mad and upset."

"You are already learning the way of love, the love that you create within."

"But I hardly have any," sighs the little girl, pressing her hands upon her heart. "And what am I supposed to do with it? The others are cold and not my friends."

"You can bring your idea of love to them."

"But how can I give an idea? I don't understand!"

"It's much easier than you may think. It involves only two steps. When you're with someone, you must first create the idea of love within yourself. Then just get into the moment with the other person. That's all you do."

"But the moment is for when I am alone!" argues the little girl.

"It also offers a gift for being with others."

"But I don't know how!"

"It's not difficult, Amanda. You just open your senses to the person you are with. See them, hear them, be with them."

"How?"

"Maybe you will just say hello or look at what they are looking at, or just remain a quiet presence. Or you may talk with them."

"No!" cries the little girl. "I am too afraid."

"You will find a way to be with other people that feels comfortable to you. Then you can practice it on someone."

"Like who?" challenges the little girl.

"Like anybody—the person who collects your ticket on the bus or brings the laundry or just about anybody. Just think of the love you have inside and be completely <u>with</u> that person."

"But I'm too scared around people to do anything like that," cries the little girl. "And what if they are mean!"

"You get strength from the idea of love which you create," says the swan.

"I don't feel strong," says the little girl.

"Maybe not yet," answers the swan, "but is your idea of love getting stronger? That is the important thing."

The little girl looks down upon the ground and hugs her knees. "I don't know," she says.

"Can you tell me what your idea of love is about so far, Amanda?"

She pauses for a while. "Caring," she finally says softly. "And not being mean," she adds a little louder. "And not leaving people when they don't want you to!" She looks into the eyes of her swan. "That's about all."

"It is a strong idea, Amanda. It comes from inside your sacred place where no wounders are allowed. Its strength is pure and its warmth is real."

"If it is, then tell me," pleads the little girl. She takes the woman's hand in hers and presses the other against her heart. "Tell me what happened to your mate. You said you would if I could get love."

The swan looks at the little girl. "You are right, Amanda. I feel the warmth of your caring all the way out in the water," says the swan, "so I will tell you my story." He makes a complete circle in the water, lifts his head and begins. "When my mate left me it was for another."

"Oh!" she sighs, now with both hands upon her heart. "Oh, how sad."

"A magnificent swan emerged one day from the distance, looming above me. He began to dance across the water. He had the greatest wing span and raced fiercer than the wind. His skidding and screeching aroused great attention. When his mating dance was over, my mate left with him."

"What did you do?"

"I was left broken and ashamed, forced to escape with my life."

"Is that when you came here?" asks the little girl.

"Yes, Amanda.   When I first arrived in these distant waters, I tried to seek refuge among the white swans.   But their squawking disturbed me and I cowered at their displays of scorn. I swam out to the deepest waters and faced my separateness. Out there alone, I realized how powerful was this force of love—not in what it had taken from me but in what it had given. I knew I wanted love to grow again inside my own heart."

The little girl nods understanding toward her swan.

"I spent many hours with this idea and held onto it, even as the others rejected me," continues the swan. "Soon there was no one to object to the warmth that I began to radiate and many to swim within its range, to bask unknowingly in its radiance."

"Then how come I can't see it?" asks the little girl.

"It is very quiet," says the swan, "but powerful." He glides toward the water's edge and looks directly into the eyes of the little girl. "It is working right now, Amanda."

She gazes back at her beautiful swan.

"Generate love, Amanda. I will always be here to share its warmth," he says, beginning his turn. "Be sure to practice it with others in the meantime, will you?" With a swoop of his neck, the swan makes his way through the flock of white swans and beyond them.

Lesson ten

One day the little girl sees a fragile and intricately colored moth flickering across the meadow. She loves the way it appears and disappears. She chases it from here to there and back again, careful not to scare her delicate friend. Suddenly it reposes momentarily right before her. She is filled with admiration for its beauty and its pulse of life. When it finally flies off, the little girl returns to the old stone house, feeling the strength of her own heart beating.

That evening, she decides to venture forth on her first outing with the other children. She will tag along quietly, attempting not to attract attention, but feeling strong enough to mingle within the group.

The group, led by teachers, walks down to the docks to experience a brisk autumn evening.

Suddenly one of the children shouts, "Look! There's a black swan!"

Sure enough, the little girl's beautiful black swan can be seen in the distance with two white swans gracefully turning this way and that in the water near the docks.

Her stomach tightens into a knot as the children begin pointing and gesturing toward the spectacular sight. She can't believe that other people—other children—can see her special friend.

"Look! Look!" they all begin shouting in excitement.

Jonathan is the first to run over to the swan. The teachers guide the rest of the children toward the docks to get a closer look. The little girl is pulled along, but she is very afraid, silent among her companions. The knot in her stomach tightens.

A large boat suddenly arrives at the other side of the dock. The captain calls to his son, "Look! There's the black swan!" The boy throws bread into the water. He is trying to attract the magnificent black swan and his companions. But it is only the white swans who rush to dip low into the water and swim under the dock. They come up on the other side and take up the bread in their beaks.

The black swan remains behind.

The little girl doesn't take her eyes off her beautiful

swan. She notices he is quivering. He has made several attempts to dip his head under the dock, but can't get low enough to swim underneath and get to the other side. Each time he is unsuccessful, he comes up quivering and moving his head about. Then he tries again but seems unable to brave the murky waters beneath the low beams of the dock.

"The black one is afraid!" shouts Jonathan.

"He's afraid!" the other children join in calling out. "The black swan is afraid!"

The two white swans are swooping up the bread with their beaks but soon turn around to look for the black swan. They see him off on the other side of the dock struggling. They quickly swim back under the docks toward him.

They get on either side and show him how to dip lower into the water. It takes many efforts, but eventually they help him swim underneath the docks and make it to the other side.

The black swan quickly swims to the bread, takes some up in his beak and lifts his long beautiful neck to swallow. Afterward, he glides away from the man and the boat and the other swans, avoiding the dock altogether, streaming past his companions and all the way out to the deepest waters.

The little girl is angry and also worried. She is confused about the black swan.

The next day the woman is supposed to take the little girl to the water's edge. She waits anxiously for the promised time, anxious to ask the black swan about the disturbing scene at the docks. Maybe the black swan isn't anybody after all, worries the little girl. Maybe she is no one and no one is anyone, she wonders. The confusion is swirling in her head and the waiting, as usual, is unbearable.

Finally amidst thoughts and worries bobbing about in her mind, she feels the woman's warm hand and soft voice. "Come precious one," says the woman.

The little girl is still nervous as she watches the black swan materialize out of the mist over the water and glide gracefully into view. "How are you, Amanda," he asks, as always.

She lifts her face to the breeze and feels the skirts of the woman softly fluttering at her knees. "I saw you at the water!" challenges the little girl. "You were afraid. Afraid to go under the docks. The other swans had to help you."

"That is so," says the swan.

"But you are the black swan and you are strong and brave."

"I don't have any special strength and bravery," says the swan. "No more than I need. No more than you have, Amanda."

"But you must be stronger and braver than I am!" cries the little girl.

"Why must that be so?" asks the swan.

"Because you are supposed to know what to do and how to be!"

"I am practicing how to use the moment, just as you are," explains the black swan.

"But I'm not good at it," says the little girl, shaking her head back and forth, very upset. "And I need you to be strong so you can help me."

"It's not about special strength, Amanda. It's about remembering to stay in the moment. We lose the moment because we get distracted—distracted by grief of what's passed or fear of what's coming. The past and future both have a powerful pull. They keep pulling us out of the present. But when we catch that happening, we just take hold and return to the moment so that we can practice what we know."

"But I can't do that by myself! And who are you to give advice!" chastises the little girl. "You couldn't even swim under the docks by yourself. You were afraid!"

The beautiful swan lifts his wings in the water and smiles upon the little girl. "My moment slips away from me just like yours does. That's why I must practice it over and over. You saw me after I took the bread. I swam all the way out to the deepest waters," reminds the swan. "I went there to regain the moment, find my center, celebrate my existence."

"But I still have too many bad feelings to do that," insists the little girl.

"Life has a way of bringing difficult feelings, Amanda. They are part of its currents. But you know how to use your tools to find the moment and start fresh each time."

"I keep forgetting to."

"We all keep forgetting to. But we have our feelings to remind us. When you have a bad feeling, Amanda, just go back to the moment and practice what you know."

"But I don't know anything!" challenges the little girl.

"Of course you do, Amanda. You are learning so many things—how to find your center and keep it safe, how to find the moment and accept your separateness, how to face your reality and discover the importance of being alive, and how to treat others with love." The swan swirls in the water.

The little girl feels a strong breeze. She wraps her arms around herself.

"Yes, Amanda. Gather your arms around yourself to gather together all that you know. Then the moment will be yours. You own it. Only you can command it." The swan swoops his head into the water and begins his turn, gliding gracefully to the distant horizon.

Lesson eleven

The days are growing short. Breezes begin to blow across the meadows and through the trees. The air is crisp, the grasses tall and dry. The little girl is on the lawn, watching the Canadian geese at play. She is waiting for her next appointment with the woman. She gathers her arms around herself as she waits and worries and hopes for the woman to come. There, feeling the heat of the afternoon sun, she sees the woman finally arrive through the great doors, her skirts blowing in the breeze. The little girl runs to greet her.

As they walk along, she pulls the woman's hand toward the orchard which stands in the distance. Thousands of red apples dot the green landscape. The woman follows along, entering through a row of trees with the little girl. They venture further alone, down the long orchard rows draped in red apples and mint green leaves, and on into the forest, keeping hold of each other's hand.

"Are you afraid, precious one?" asks the woman, as they walk though the tangled web of branches laden with ripening fruit.

"Yes," says the little girl. "But I am going anyway."

Soon they are in the densest woods.

At once they come to a giant rock. Its sharp edges glisten in sunlight sparkling through the canopy of leaves.

"Can you lift me up?" asks the little girl.

The woman complies, setting her firmly atop its cold hard surface. "I will be right down here at the base of the rock," says the woman. "I will be here if you need me."

The little girl watches the woman take her seat on the ground and lean against the rock, spreading out her skirts. She feels the soft material fluttering against her dangling feet.

And then, through the foliage, the little girl sees flashes of red. It gets brighter and brighter and nearer and nearer.

"Daddy!" calls the little girl.

Her father appears out of the thicket. "Hello, Mandy," he says.

"Where have you been, Daddy?" she asks, gathering her arms around herself.

"Nearby," he says. "Why don't you come home, Mandy?" He attempts to take her hand. "We're waiting for you."

"You left me on the rock!" challenges the little girl.

"It is time for you to come with me," says her father.

"I'm not going with you," says the little girl.

"But I'm here to take you," he says and slides his hand up her legs to her knees.

"I don't want to go with you," she insists. "I don't want you to harm me anymore."

"I won't harm you, Mandy. Come with me," says her daddy and caresses her knees.

"No, I won't let you harm me again," she replies. "Please leave me alone."

"Come with me, Mandy."

"I will stay where I am."

"Nonsense," says her daddy. "You must come with me. You can't stay here all alone."

"I will not be alone. I can take care of myself."

With that, her daddy begins to fade backward, his face becoming the last thing she sees before the red of his shirt disappears in the thicket.

"I still love you, Daddy," she calls, the tears welling up in her eyes, making the world appear swollen and magnified.

She soon feels the woman's skirts gently blowing against her ankles. She beckons to be lifted off the rock, taking the woman's hand. Her knees feel weak where her father's fingers had lingered.

The woman helps to steady the little girl. They slowly make their way, arm in arm, through the forest and out of the orchard. Soon they arrive at the slope.

They descend to the water quickly. The little girl feels her chest pounding hard. The black swan is waiting for them as they arrive.

"I know I can't be with my daddy!" she cries, "and it hurts in my heart!" Tears fall down her face and onto the sand, flowing and flowing.

The black swan looks upon the little girl who is crying on the shoreline. He waits until her sobs subside. Then he opens his magnificent wings and reveals for the first time, white tipped feathers on the underside.

The little girl gazes upon him.

"You are learning to own your own life, Amanda," he says, "and that is good."

She shakes her head. "What good is owning it?" she finally answers. "I don't like my life."

"Life is a miracle," says the swan, fluttering his beautifully tipped wings.

The little girl's eyes open wide. "I try to believe in miracles," she insists, "but I can't."

"It's not about believing. You just have to see what is there right in front of you to realize the miracle of life," says the swan. "Existence is all around you and you are standing in the middle of it. How and why we come into being, we can only wonder about. But we are alive within a vast, mysterious universe, infinite in scope—that much we know. For each of us, that simple truth is a miracle. Existence itself is a miracle."

"But we don't go on forever, we die," says the little girl.

"If we are only here for a while," says the swan pulling back in the water, "then we don't have time to waste. Our destiny is now."

"But I can't bear mine. I was left by my parents—alone on a rock to die."

"Your reality is difficult, to be sure. But accepting its challenge will help you grow bigger. You will grow a bigger sense of yourself, Amanda, grow so big that your problems become just a small part of you. Then they can't harm you as much. You will grow to a place beyond your problems."

"How am I supposed to do that?"

"Through your imagination, as always, Amanda, and I will help you. It's a special exercise, one you must begin to practice every day."

"Doing what?" she queries.

"Getting into the split second of the moment and

giving your mind a special time every day to expand."

The little girl shakes her head and wrinkles her face in confusion. "Expand?"

"Expand your scope all the way out to the universe," says the swan.

"What does the universe have to do with it?" she challenges.   "It doesn't have a mind like we do, does it?"

"Some questions don't have answers," says the swan, fluttering his wings. "But the universe does exist—that much you can know, just by knowing that you are here now.   If you exist, you are part of the universe.   Part and particle of its energy.   Just a speck perhaps.   But as you open yourself to how vast it all is, you realize it is yours to behold."

"This doesn't help me."

"Realizing you are part of the universe helps you think beyond the walls of troubles."

"But how can this work if the universe doesn't even think and do things?"

"YOU have a mind. It is your own work that does it."

"Does what?"

"Helps you grow bigger than your problems, get to a place beyond where you are now."

"How am I supposed to do this?"

"By spending some special time every day letting your mind go in and out."

"In and out of what?"

"You go into the center of yourself and out to the expanse of the universe and back again."

"This doesn't make any sense!" exclaims the little girl. "How come other people don't have to do this?"

"Throughout time, many others have been doing this very thing."

"Why?" demands the little girl.

"They are attempting to fathom what it means to exist within an infinite universe."

"Well, I've never seen them do it!" challenges the little girl.

"Now you will begin to notice the many different ways people have of doing it."

"Like how?"

"Some gaze at the sky or speak their feelings right out loud. Some close their eyes and press their hands together. Some relax and let their minds wander. Some ask for things. Some climb to mountaintops or kneel down in temples. Some focus on something to drown out all other thoughts and distractions. Some become scientists and explore all that they can find. Some form pictures in their minds of what they want. Some meet with others and ask questions. Others seek silence and solitude."

"Why are they doing this?" asks the little girl.

"Reality is vast and mysterious. People are always

trying to figure out where it comes from and why it is like it is. With our eyes, we can only bend a fraction of its light rays; with our ears, we can only receive a narrow band of its vibrations, and with our minds, we can only form ideas about its essence.   We can only attempt to grasp it, each in our own special ways."

"What is the point?" demands the little girl.   "Why do people bother to do it?"

"To get beyond where they are now."

"I still don't understand," complains the little girl.

"That is because you don't know where to begin, and I will help you now. I will help you learn to use the vastness of the universe as a way of bringing hope. Are you ready?"

The little girl nods, but her face does not let go of its strain.

"Close your eyes, Amanda, and pretend.   Imagine that the universe is so vast and reality so unknowable, that everything you can possibly want is possible—if you are open to it."

"But I don't have what I want!" counters the little girl.

"That may be true. But think about what you want out of life if you could have anything you wanted.   These thoughts bring pleasure to the mind. They are gifts from your imagination. Think about what you wish to have and do. Pretend it is all possible, just waiting for you to go find it."

"But this isn't true."

"It doesn't have to be true." says the swan. "Imagining it helps your mind grow."

"Even if you don't believe it?" queries the little girl.

"You don't have to believe it. Pretending nurtures your mind. Just let go and imagine that all you want can come to you in its own time, from somewhere within or without."

The little girl's face begins to relax, her eyelids resting gently closed.

"What if all I want is for my family to come back?" she asks.

"It is important to remember," cautions the swan, "that as you use your imagination, you must always move forward rather than backward, toward real possibility. Always favor reality."

"But all I want is my family!" implores the little girl. "And they are not here."

"Moving toward possibility means it must hinge upon yourself and not upon the actions of others outside of your control. Think within these boundaries," says the swan. "Tell me what else you want in life," he continues. "Go with reality; it is bountiful enough as it is. Think about what would make your life better and tell me."

"A whole apple pie just for me!" she shouts gleefully.

The swan smiles upon the little girl. "That's a good

start, Amanda."

"Will I get it just by imagining?"

"Some things you will, some you may not. Some involve a lot of work, some great patience, others, luck. Whether or not you get all you imagine, the important thing is that it is possible. Live your life now, realizing all is possible. Continue imagining, Amanda.   What else might you want?"

She takes a deep breath. "To be happy."

"Of course. And tell me in what way."

"I want to be with people who care about me and never leave me." The little girl looks at the sky and adds. "And in case they go away, I want to be strong and for there to always be other people who care."

"All of that is moving toward real possibility, Amanda. Keep sharpening your idea of what you want and who you are becoming. Feel grateful to be alive and part of the universe—to be receiving so much within it. This will help you expand and your problems to shrink."

" Just by imagining?"

"Yes," says the swan. "You already know that the universe goes on forever. Just as your imagination does. They are alike in many ways—each composed of energy and endless possibility.   Think of the infinite universe and imagine that you are its grateful child. Imagine that what you ask for is possible, if not now, later. Be grateful for the hope this thought brings."

"I know I can't do this!" insists the little girl. "I'm too upset. I have no hope. Why should I be grateful that I live in a residence for children?"

"And there, in that very place, you can find the special time and place to think about what you want," says the swan. "Fill your heart with gratitude for all of the blessings you are creating."

The little girl gazes at her swan. "This is too hard," she says.

"You have your imagination and your capacity for love—all that you need," answers the swan. "I will wait as long as it takes for you to discover the possibility of life and to find the gifts within and around you. You must find a quiet time and practice every day," he says, pulling back in the water and fluttering his wings.

"I don't want to wait so long to see you. I miss you too much," she says, lifting her gaze toward the horizon.

"If you make your quiet time come first in your life," the swan reassures her, "you will notice changes sooner than you think. They will appear in your everyday life, and I will be right here, waiting to share them with you. "

The swan lifts his majestic neck. He makes his turn and glides gracefully through the flock of white swans, out to the most distant waters.

Lesson twelve

Some of the trees near the old stone house are already standing in pools of red and yellow leaves fallen at their feet. The little girl is wading through them, listening to the rustling and crackling, the sounds of autumn leaves getting crunched underfoot. She is also thinking about Jonathan who is walking beside her. She feels unsettled. She has waited a long time for her next appointment with the woman. This time, she is going to take Jonathan with her to see the black swan.

The woman with soft flowing skirts finally arrives and they quickly take the shortcut through the orchard burgeoning with apples. Many have fallen.

They reach the final slope where the little girl pauses. "You stay here for a minute, Jonathan. I'll be right back, okay?"

The woman's soft skirts flutter softly in the breeze as she walks a few steps ahead.

"Okay," says the boy, throwing a stone against the tree.

"I just have to talk to someone," explains the little girl, pointing to the shoreline.

"Yeah," he says, and throws another stone.

The little girl runs to the woman's side and they make their way to the shoreline. The black swan is already waiting, turning gracefully in the water to face her. "How is your practicing, Amanda?" asks her beautiful swan.

"Everyday, I take special time," she reports proudly. "But I have a question. What do we do about Jonathan? He got mad on visitor's day and broke the window. Now he's in lots of trouble and he's crying all the time."

The swan swoops close to the little girl and gently touches her outstretched hand with the brilliant red of his beak. "Why not share what you've learned with him, Amanda?"

"Me?" asks the little girl, her eyes brightening at the unexpected touch of the swan. "But the boy is so upset and crying all the time," she explains.

"He's not alone in his pain, Amanda, just as you are not alone in yours. There are always people who suffer great torment. But we are here to help each other."

"I don't know how to help Jonathan."

"Begin at the beginning. Let him see how you find your center and keep it safe inside," suggests the swan. "Show him the path."

"I still have bad feelings of my own," says the little girl. "I can't help somebody else! I was hoping you would talk to him for me."

"It is not necessary, Amanda.   You can help him yourself. Show him the steps you have taken."

"How?"

"Begin at the beginning.   Let him know he is not alone. Just as you are not alone in learning how to experience life.   It is a great gift.   But it is not yours to take; it is yours to give. It is the moment.   Help others find it.   And love them, Amanda, as you are learning to love life."

"What if I help Jonathan?   I'm afraid he will be mean to me someday. He will throw me away."

"You can't be thrown away.   You can only give yourself away, Amanda.   And even if you do, you can always return to your center and find yourself again and create love all over again."

"I still need someone to love me," implores the little girl to her friend.

"Of course you do.   And if you take time everyday to imagine receiving what you want, you will have what you want—including someone special.   You will have other loving people as well, if it is what you are imagining and wanting. But remember that you are a source of love yourself, Amanda.   Feel its warmth and let it shine outward. Give yourself fully to the moment and each moment will be love. It will be a journey, always in the present," says the swan. "You will find it. You have the whole universe to explore, within and without."

"I have to go now," says the little girl. "I don't want to keep Jonathan waiting. He might be worried." She turns and runs back up the slope.

The woman unfolds her arms and dusts herself off as the breeze catches her skirts. "It is she who has trouble waiting," says the woman standing before the great swan. "She gets a knot in her stomach when she waits."

"Yes," says the swan. "And you must never keep her waiting, Amanda."   He makes a full turn in the water. "Never wait. Her wounds are real. The moment is always now. She is your heart. Take good care of her."

"Yes," says the woman, as she opens her arms to watch the swan glide out to the deepest waters and slowly disappear over the horizon. She remains for a while. Then she walks back up the slope and into the apple orchard to gather its fruit—enough to make an apple pie.

Ending is a new beginning

I wrote this story during the summer of 1994 with both a camera and pen. I was captivated by the sight of the graceful black swan sailing through the harbor. Two white swans were often seen trailing behind him and other swans made room for his passage. He often swam out beyond them to the furthest reaches of the harbor. I trailed the mysterious presence of the black swan for two months before I saw him lift his wings and reveal the white tips of his feathers underneath. A few times he approached the shoreline and extended his brilliant red beak within feet of where I stood. Once I saw him afraid to swim under the docks, being helped by white swans. So isolated and so alive—he conveyed a message of hope and renewal. I never found out what brought him all the way here from Australia to be immersed in solitude, vulnerable within a new landscape, or where he flew away to at the end of the summer. But during his presence, he helped me to reach to the center of the pain and discover a wellspring of healing.

The twelve lessons of recovery are the culmination of

over twenty years of helping people overcome heartbreak, loss, and abandonment. The lessons follow a clinically-tested sequence. They provide a protocol for healing the woundedness of abandonment, a supplement for therapy. By practicing them on a daily basis, we gain from our experiences no matter how painful they are, and find greater love and life than before.

Recovery is an active process, one that requires our full participation. Let this book be your resource and guide, providing inspiration and example for performing the exercises. Not everyone is expected to relate to all of them. Some lessons will resonate more with one person than another, depending on each person's unique response to life.

There are elements set into the story to help your recovery along, which many readers tend to overlook on their first reading. For instance, the little girl makes a gesture during each of the lessons with the black swan:

First exercise—finding your center—*she closes her eyes and places her hands on her chest* to signify that she is burrowing deep within to discover the center of her being.

Second exercise—cleansing the wound—*she turns her hands outward* to show that she is pushing the wounder out to create a sacred place within.

Third exercise—remaining present—*she tilts her head to the side* indicating that she is attentive to background sounds— her way of bringing in the moment.

Fourth exercise—facing your separateness—*she lifts her face* to signify that she is a separate person, able to stand on her own.

Fifth exercise—welcoming your existence—*she lifts her chest* to show that she appreciates the importance of her own life.

Sixth exercise—accepting the unchangeable—*she takes a breath* to summon the strength it takes to face her reality.

Seventh exercise—increasing your capacity for love—*she presses her palms on her chest* to signify she is able to generate warmth from within.

Eighth exercise—letting others be who they are—*she turns her palm upward* to show her openness.

Ninth exercise—giving to give, not get—*she puts one hand on her heart, reaches outward with the other* to show she is ready to extend her warmth.

Tenth exercise—embracing the new self—*she puts her arms around herself* to convey that she is gathering together all she has learned and taking it within her.

Eleventh exercise—placing yourself in the larger picture—*she gazes skyward* to signify that she is looking for meaning and purpose, seeking greater destiny.

Twelfth exercise—making a connection—*she stands up, arms outstretched* to show she is ready to share love with another. (See Appendix A)

These gestures help to make the lessons easier to remember when you are out in the world caught up in life. Having read the story, you may wish to go back to the text to reflect upon the application of the lessons. The black swan carefully explains how to practice each one. As the girl applies them to her life, she discovers significant changes. As we follow her progress, we glimpse the benefit the exercises can have in our lives as well.

As we practice the twelve lessons, they begin to flow into one another. The first three create an *internal center*. The next four lay in the cornerstones for building a *new sense of self*. The next two (eight and nine) *enhance our connection to others*. Then come eleven and twelve which lead to *owning and transcending*, and the last lesson helps us make a new connection to *greater love and life*. (See Appendix B)

For most people, just reading the story for enjoyment will not produce the personal changes they are hoping to find. If you wish to truly benefit, you must apply the exercises to your life. They provide a recipe for a new way of being. With practice, they become one flowing gesture: At once you are centered, present, accepting life's challenge, grateful to be alive, and deeply connected.

For those interested in setting up abandonment support groups in your area, finding out what services and products are available on the subject, or seeking further information about the twelve lessons and other related concerns, please contact my website: **www.abandonmentrecovery.com**.

The Long-Islander.

Founded by Walt Whitman in 1838

Huntington's Newspaper of Record for over 150 years

ar. No. 7   Thursday July 28, 1993   50 Cents

G'Day Swan

If birds could talk, we might know what this Australian Black Swan (Cygnus Atratus) is doing in local waters. The bird, which is black with white flight feathers and a red beak, was preening when Huntington resident Ellen Klaffky took this photograph near Mill Dam marina.   Photo by Ellen Klaffky

Appendix A

GESTURES

Lesson 1: centering	close eyes, hands across chest
Lesson 2: cleansing	turn hands outward from chest
Lesson 3: creating presence	tilt head to side
Lesson 4: separating	lift face
Lesson 5: welcoming	lift chest
Lesson 6: accepting	take breath
Lesson 7: increasing	press palms on heart
Lesson 8: letting	open one hand
Lesson 9: giving	extend open hand
Lesson 10: embracing	arms around self
Lesson 11: transcending	gaze skyward
Lesson 12: loving	stand up, arms outstretched

Appendix B

INTEGRATING THE TWELVE EXERCISES

SELF	Lesson 1: centering
	Lesson 2: cleansing
	Lesson 3: creating presence
INTEGRITY	Lesson 4: separating
	Lesson 5: welcoming
	Lesson 6: accepting
	Lesson 7: increasing love
RELATIONSHIP	Lesson 8: letting
	Lesson 9: giving
PURPOSE	Lesson 10: owning and embracing
	Lesson 11: transcending
LOVE	Lesson 12: connecting

ABOUT THE AUTHOR

Photograph by Marcia Gerardi
Print by Peter Moriority

Susan Anderson is a psychotherapist who specializes in helping people with loss, heart-break, and abandonment. In addition to her work with adults for over twenty years, she has spent the past decade researching and helping children who were in the throes of loss and disconnection and developing start-up programs for the adult community to promote awareness and strengthen emotional bonds within the family.

She runs abandonment recovery workshops and conducts seminars and lectures on related topics, and has appeared on radio and television. She is author of *The Journey from Abandonment to Healing (March 2000, Penguin Putnam)* which identifies the five stages of abandonment and provides case examples of people going through this life-changing experience. She has also authored numerous articles for journals as well as Internet distribution and **www.abandonmentrecovery.com**. She lives with her family in Huntington, New York.

In BLACK SWAN, Anderson reaches out to people across the abandonment spectrum to promote healing. Her programs are designed to help those going through the painful ending of a relationship, those experiencing chronic heartache and insecurity, and those struggling to bring love into their lives.

Susan Anderson
c/o Rock Foundations Press
P.O. Box 2307— Suite B
Huntington, New York 11743-2307
abandonment@erols.com
www.abandonmentrecovery.com
Orders: 1.800.247.6553   Fax: 516.421.6340

~ BLACK SWAN ~
QUICK ORDER FORM

Please fill out the form below before ordering to expedite the process.

Telephone orders: 1-800-247-6553 (CREDIT CARD ONLY)
Or Fax orders to: 516-421-6340 (CREDIT CARD ONLY)
Or Email your order to: abandonment@erols.com (CREDIT CARD ONLY)

Or mail your order to:
Rock Foundations Press
P.O. Box 2307-Suite B
Huntington, New York 11743-2307

YOUR NAME _____

STREET ADDRESS _____

CITY _____ STATE _____

COUNTRY _____ ZIP _____

TELEPHONE _____ email ADDRESS _____

SALES TAX: Please add the applicable sales tax for products shipped within New York State.
SHIPPING: Within the United States: Please add U.S. $5 for the 1st book or tape and $2.50 for each additional product. International: $10.00 for the 1st book or tape, $5 for each additional product.

PAYMENT METHOD:　　☐ Check　　☐ Credit Card:

☐ Visa　☐ MasterCard　☐ Optima　☐ American Express　☐ Discover

Account Number ☐☐☐☐☐☐☐☐☐☐☐☐☐☐☐☐☐☐☐☐

Expiration Date ☐☐☐☐

Cardholder'sBilling Address(if different from shipping address)_____

_____

Signature (as appears on card)_____

Print Name (as shown on card)_____

rock foundations press